First World War
and Army of Occupation
War Diary
France, Belgium and Germany

66 DIVISION
199 Infantry Brigade
Manchester Regiment
2/7th Battalion
1 September 1915 - 10 February 1916

WO95/3145/1

The Naval & Military Press Ltd
www.nmarchive.com
Published in association with The National Archives

Published by

The Naval & Military Press Ltd

Unit 10 Ridgewood Industrial Park,

Uckfield, East Sussex,

TN22 5QE England

Tel: +44 (0) 1825 749494

www.naval-military-press.com

www.nmarchive.com

This diary has been reprinted in facsimile from the original. Any imperfections are inevitably reproduced and the quality may fall short of modern type and cartographic standards.

© **Crown Copyright**
Images reproduced by permission of The National Archives, London, England, 2015.

Contents

Document type	Place/Title	Date From	Date To
Heading	WO95/3145/2/7 Battalion Manchester Regiment		
War Diary	Crowborough Camp	14/09/1915	14/09/1915
War Diary	Burham Camp	01/09/1915	19/09/1915
War Diary	Crowborough	20/09/1915	10/02/1916
Miscellaneous	Statement In Accordance With Central Force Circular Memo. Number 468	20/09/1914	20/09/1914

WO 95/3145/1

2/h Batteria Mondoshn Rognier

2/7th Battalion Manchester Regiment.   "A"

Army Form C.2118.

199/66

WAR DIARY or
INTELLIGENCE Summary.

Hour, Date, Place.	Summary of Events and Information.	Remarks and reference to Appendices.
Crowborough Camp. Sept.14th/15.	4 Mules and 1 Light Draught Horse received.	
Burham Camp. Sept.1st to 19th.	Entrenching on South London Defences.	
Crowborough. Sept.20th.	Battalion returned to Crowborough.	
" Sept.27th.	Four Field Kitchens received.	
" Sept.29th.	One 2nd.Lieut.proceeded overseas to join 1/7th Battn.Manchester Regiment.	
" Sept.30th.	Bivouacked night at Buckhurst Park.	

The Camp,
Crowborough,
Sussex.

4th October 1915.

[signature]
Colonel,
Comdg. 2/7th Battalion Manchester Regiment.

2/7th Battalion Manchester Regiment.

"A"

199/66   Army Form C.2118.

WAR DIARY or
INTELLIGENCE Summary.

Hour, Date, Place.	Summary of Events and Information.	Remarks and reference to Appendices.
Crowborough Camp.		
October 4th 1915.	Draft of two subalterns proceeded to join 1/7th Bn. Manchester Regiment, Egypt.	
October 6th 1915.	Brigade Route March.	First occasion on which travelling kitchens were used on the march. Very successful.
October 11th 1915.	Brigade Manoeuvres - "The Attack".	
October 18th 1915.	Brigade Manoeuvres - "The Attack".	
October 18th 1915.	Period of Individual Training commenced.	
November 2nd 1915.	Inspection of Transport by General Landon, Chief Inspector Q.M.G.Services.	The transport of this Battalion was specially mentioned for the excellence of its turnout.

Crowborough Camp,
Sussex.
4th November 1915.

John S Rowbotham
Capt.
for Colonel,
Comdg. 2/7th Battn Manchester Regiment.

2/7th Battalion Manchester Regiment.

"A".

Army Form C.2118.

WAR DIARY or
INTELLIGENCE SUMMARY.

Hour, Date, Place.	Summary of Events & Information.	Remarks and references to Appendices.
CROWBOROUGH CAMP.		
Nov. 9th 1915.	Received One Water Cart Mk.V. 1915.	
Nov. 11th 1915.	Received one H.D.Horse.	Establishment of Horses & Mules completed.
Nov. 11th 1915.	Received Six Wagons, G.S. Mk X.	
Nov. 11th 1915.	Inspected by Supt. of Gymnasia.	This Battalion was specially mentioned for the excellance of Physical Training & brilliancy of Bayonet Fighting.
Nov. 12th 1915.	Received Nine Sets of Pack Saddlery.	Completion.
Nov. 18th 1915.	Inspected by Major General E.T.Dickson.	Dirty condition of clothing noted. Fresh supply received following day, and issued immediately.
Nov. 25th 1915.	Received one Officers' Mess Cart.	
Dec. 1st 1915.	Establishment of Officers temporarily reduced to 23. Surplus (3) reposted to Third Line.	Authority War Office Letter 9/Infantry/2 (T.F.3.) dated 8th November 1915.

Crowborough Camp,
Sussex.
3rd December 1915.

[signature]
Colonel,
Commdg; 2/7th Battalion Manchester Regiment.

199/60 "A"

Army Form C.2118.

2/7th Battalion Manchester Regiment.

WAR DIARY or
INTELLIGENCE Summary.

Hour, Date, Place.	Summary of Events and Information.	Remarks and reference to Appendices.
Crowborough Dec. 11th 1915	Inspection by G.O.C. 66th (East Lancs) Division.	
Dec. 17th 1915	Christmas leave commenced	

Crowborough.
Sussex.
4th January 1916.

Ian D Rocell
Colonel.
Commdg. 2/7th Battalion Manchester Regiment.

199/66 "A"

2/7th Battalion Manchester Regiment.

WAR DIARY OF INTELLIGENCE SUMMARY.

Hour, Date, Place.	Summary of Events and Information.	Remarks and reference to Appendices.
Crowborough Camp.		
10-30 am. January 6th 1916.	Inspection of Transport by Lieut.-Colonel Mackenzie.	Generally good.
1-0 pm. 21st January 1916.	Inspection of Camp by Surgeon-General J.C.Culling, D.D.M.S.	There is no adverse criticism to be made throughout the whole Battalion. The kitchens, messing huts and sleeping huts were remarkably clean and satisfactory.

Ian D Reed
Comdg. 2/7th Battn. Manchester Regiment.
Colonel,

Crowborough Camp,
Sussex.
4th February 1916.

WAR DIARY
or
INTELLIGENCE SUMMARY

Army Form C. 2118.

(Erase heading not required.)

Hour, Date, Place	Summary of Events and Information	Remarks and references to Appendices
CROWBOROUGH		
12.0 a.m. Feb 2nd 1916	Inspection of 1st line transport by the O.C.	The known out were excellente but more attention might be paid to detail by the R.T.O.
8.30 a.m. Feb 3rd 1916	Classification test of Signallers by O.C. Div'l Signallers	All men entered (16) passed doubt officials result of all concerned
10.30 a.m. Feb 7th 1916	Battalion and horse inspection by Colonel Commanding the 199th Infantry Brigade	Rapid "Good" Consider as horses best Seen Latham Recall Good Peavell Steward & Marsaul
9.0 a.m. Feb 10th 1916	Battalion inspected by Inspector of Gymnasia at Physical Drill and Bayonet fighting	

signature
COLONEL
Comdg. 2/7th Battalion MANCHESTER REGT.

Statement in accordance with
Central Force Circular memo. Number 468
Dated 20th September 1914.

UNIT. 2/7th Battalion Manchester Regiment.

BRIGADE. 199th Infantry Brigade.

DIVISION. 66th (East Lancashire) Division.

MOBILIZATION
CENTRE. Manchester.

TEMPORARY
WAR STATION Crowborough.

(a) MOBILIZATION. Nil.

(b) CONCENTRATION
AT WAR STATION. Nil.

(c) ORGANISATION FOR DEFENCE. This Battalion is armed with 600 Japanese Rifles.
The Transport shown in A.O. 9 Gen.No.4696 dated 3rd January 1915 is very incomplete.

(d) TRAINING. The opportunities the ground affords for training is being taken advantage of to the fullest extent.
The Junior Officers and senior N.C.O's have derived much benefit from the course of instruction under Major E.H.Hummel, the Divisional Drill Instructor.

(e) DISCIPLINE. General Conduct Good.

(f) ADMINISTRATION.

(1) MEDICAL SERVICES. There is no Maltese Cart and no Medical or Surgical Equipment (panniers emergency boxes).

(2) VETERINARY SERVICES. Satisfactory.

(3) SUPPLY SERVICE. Satisfactory.

(4) TRANSPORT SERVICES. The Transport available is 1 Civilian wagon, 1 Water Cart, 7 S.A.A.Carts, 7 Horses & 15 Mules. (L.D.II) 8 Horses (H.D.) and 9 Mules (pack) 6 sets of double harness have been received

(5) ORDNANCE SERVICES. Supplies cannot be obtained for the following, requisitions for which have been constantly made :-
Alphabet letters for marking identity discs.
Rifle Slings.
Machine Guns.
Mekometers.

(6) BILLETS.   Nil.
It is exceedingly insatisfactory that the Officers have all to live away from the Camp. They occupy two houses, one a quarter of an hour's walk away, and the other twenty minutes. There is also not sufficient accomodation for the full complement of Officers.

(7) CHANNELS OF CORRESPONDENCE.

(8) RANGE CONSTRUCTION.

(9) SUPPLY OF REMOUNTS. The remounts in possession are 10 for Officers, 8 Heavy Draught horses, and 7 Light draught horses.

(g) RE-ORGANISATION INTO HOME AND IMPERIAL SERVICE.   Nil.

(h) PREPARATION OF UNITS FOR IMPERIAL SERVICE. There are no men available for drafts under the ruling of W.O.Letter 212/5995 A.G.1. dated 26th July 1915.

John E. Rowbotham

Capt. & Adjt.
for
Colonel.
Commdg. 2/7th Battalion Manchester Regiment.

The Camp,
  Burham.

   3rd September 1915.

www.ingramcontent.com/pod-product-compliance
Lightning Source LLC
Chambersburg PA
CBHW081517160426
43193CB00014B/2723